HELPFUL PEOPLE

TEACHER

JAMIE FICKETT

NORWOOD HOUSE PRESS

Library of Congress Cataloging-in-Publication Data:

Names: Fickett, Jamie.
Title: Teacher / Jamie Fickett.
Description: Buffalo, NY : Norwood House Press, 2025. | Series: Helpful people | Includes glossary and index.
Identifiers: ISBN 9781684502981 (pbk.) | ISBN 9781684502998 (library bound) | ISBN 9781684503001 (ebook)
Subjects: LCSH: Teachers--Juvenile literature.
Classification: LCC LB1775.F535 2025 | DDC 371.1--dc23

Published in 2025 by
Norwood House Press
2544 Clinton Street
Buffalo, NY 14224

Designer: Ocean Books
Editor: Kim Thompson

Photo credits: Cover, p. 1 Chris Howey/Shutterstock.com; p. 5 Drazen Zigic/Shutterstock.com; p. 6 iofoto/Shutterstock.com; pp. 7, 21 Peopleimages/Shutterstock.com; p. 9 Jacob Kund/Shutterstock.com; p. 11 Krakenimages/Shutterstock.com; p. 12Josep Curto/Shutterstock.com; p. 13 Pixel-Shot/Shutterstock.com; p. 15 BAZA Production/Shutterstock.com; p. 16 stockfour/Shutterstock.com; p. 17 wavebreakmedia/Shutterstock.com; p. 19 michaeljung/Shutterstock.com

Printed in the United States of America

CPSIA compliance information: Batch #CW25NHP: For further information contact Norwood House Press at 1-800-237-9932.

TABLE OF CONTENTS

WHAT IS A TEACHER?

Teachers are important helpers in our **community**. They help us learn how to read. They teach us about the world we live in.

Teachers help us learn to get along with others. They teach us to share, to be kind, and to listen.

Teachers help us when we don't understand something. They keep explaining until we do understand.

Teachers make sure we are safe and happy. We can tell them when we are sad. They will help us feel better.

WHAT DOES A TEACHER WEAR?

Many teachers wear comfortable shirts with pants or skirts. Other teachers wear dresses or suits.

The PE teacher wears a T-shirt and sweatpants. The art teacher wears an apron to **protect** their clothes.

Sometimes, there are **theme** days at school. Teachers may wear pajamas on Pajama Day.

Teachers are pirates on Pirate Day. On Storybook Day, they dress as characters from books.

WHAT TOOLS DOES A TEACHER USE?

Teachers use **tools** to help us learn. They write lessons and draw pictures on **whiteboards**. This helps us understand new ideas.

I have played
playing
I had

Teachers read stories to us from books. Books help us learn about animals, places, and people.

Teachers use computers and tablets in the classroom. We can watch videos and play learning games.

HOW DO YOU BECOME A TEACHER?

Teachers go to college to study how children learn. They learn how to teach **subjects** like reading and math.

Teachers must pass a special test. Then, they get a **license** to work in a school.

Teachers know how to be kind and **patient**. They listen when students have questions or problems. Good teachers care about every student.

GLOSSARY

community (kuh-MYOO-ni-tee): a social group of any size whose members live together, have a common government, and often share the same culture or history

license (LYE-suhns): a certificate or document that officially gives permission to own something or do something

patient (PAY-shuhnt): calm and uncomplaining; able to deal with problems without getting angry or upset

protect (pruh-TEKT): to guard and keep safe from harm, attack, injury, or danger

subjects (SUHB-jekts): areas of study; branches of knowledge

theme (theem): a unifying or dominant idea

tools (toolz): pieces of equipment that you use to do a job; things that help you reach a goal

whiteboards (WITE-bordz): smooth, glossy sheets of white plastic that can be written on with special markers and then erased in the manner of a chalkboard

THINKING QUESTIONS

1. What is the job of a teacher?
2. Why does the art teacher wear an apron?
3. How is a teacher helpful to the community?
4. What are the characteristics of a good teacher?
5. Would you like to become a teacher? Why or why not?

INDEX

ABOUT THE AUTHOR

Jamie Fickett lives on Long Island, New York, where he grew up. Every Saturday he enjoys going to the Bronx Zoo and seeing the rhinos from the Wild Asia Monorail. Rhinoceroses have been his favorite animal ever since he was eight and received the nickname Rhino while playing catcher in Little League baseball.